SHADOWS AND LIGHT
Showcasing a Hosta Love Affair

WRITTEN AND PHOTOGRAPHED BY

Robert J. Zimmer

SHADOWS AND LIGHT

Showcasing a Hosta Love Affair

SHADOWS AND LIGHT

Showcasing a Hosta Love Affair

Table of Contents

Hosta Dreams, Hosta Passions

A hosta love affair.

A passionate dalliance that began nearly a decade ago when we first set eyes upon each other. It quickly blossomed into something deeper, a steamy, tumultuous journey ever since. A journey filled with adventure, excitement, obsession, danger and drama.

I began my dance with hostas in the gardens of a dear friend, subtly captivated by the colors, textures and breathtaking dimensions of the plants before me. I was captivated by the substance of the leaves. The sheer mass of gorgeous, subtle coloration that sprawled before me.

Viewing mature hostas in all their splendor and glory is quite a different experience from browsing small, potted starter plants in a garden center or nursery. Until one learns the patience and nurturing required to give rise to a spectacular specimen plant, the art of growing hostas is but an illusion.

Thankfully, there are many wonderful hosta growers and gardens in my area where it's possible to see spectacular display plants at full maturity in all of their tantalizing magnificence.

Many who first begin to garden with hostas become quite obsessive. And that's putting it mildly. All at once, we develop a crazed sense of hosta-mania. We dive deeper into the hobby as we explore new garden centers and online retailers, each with something a little bit different to keep the passion growing.

Collecting hosta comes naturally. We simply scoop up every plant we can find that does not look or sound familiar.

Thankfully, the hosta world unveils a wide range of beautiful foliage, stunning architecture, unusual textures, versatile plants and enough variety is to keep us busy for decades to come.

Often, I am asked for the name of my favorite hosta. This book represents a collection of nearly 125 of these plants, all deeply desirable. My tastes may change from season to season, week to week, even day to day. Undoubtedly, there are hundreds, if not thousands of hostas I would love to add to this list. Don't hold it against me if your favorite is not included.

Hostas provide gardeners with so many excellent plant characteristics that make them invaluable in the landscape. These plants also provide exceptional color, pattern, texture, form, substance, as well as long-lasting beauty, versatility and relative ease of care.

I've titled this book 'Shadows and Light' for many reasons. Hostas have definitely come out of the shadows over the past few decades as new trends in hybridization have resulted in a stunning new generation of hostas that only superficially resemble their commonly grown ancestors. A new spotlight shines on these dramatic plants and there appears to be no limit to what we'll be graced with as hosta breeding continues to showcase new trends and characteristics.

More than a hosta encyclopedia, my aim is to showcase the features of many of my favorite hostas and express my undying love for these incredible beauties in a way never seen before.

I hope you enjoy this collection of beautiful plants and information as I showcase a love affair with hostas.

Sincerely,

Robert J. Zimmer

One of my favorite of all hosta varieties is H. Ebb Tide, an elegant,
cascading beauty in green and flecked gold.

H. Guardian Angel, always stunning, is another of my favorite varieties.

SHOWCASING A HOSTA LOVE AFFAIR

H. *Winter Snow*

Gleaming in brilliant lime green with a crisp, snow white edge, this breathtaking beauty has become more spectacular with each passing season in my garden. A massive, variegated sport of the popular Sum and Substance, Winter Snow is a big and powerful plant, brightening shady spots or blessing garden beds with its stunning, refreshing form.

H. *Independence*

With a deep green center and wonderfully flecked edges in creamy white, this is one of my favorite plants to pair with hosta varieties that boast the opposite variegation and misting, such as Allegan Fog, Revolution and London Fog. Upon closer inspection, the border between the solid central leaf and the outer edge is not always cut and dry, but composed of several layers of green.

H. *Blizzard*

A spectacular specimen plant for sun or shade, Blizzard features variable streaking in shades of yellow and white over the lime green leaf surface with a feathery, cream to white border. In full sun, this stunning sport of H. Winter Snow is at its best, with the contrast in coloration at its most striking.

The elegant, undulating leaf edges create a beautiful effect in the garden, giving the plant an air of motion as it rises and flows over and above smaller hostas and companion plants at its feet.

H. *Journey's End*

Gorgeous coloration, heavy veining and an intense, rippled edge earn this spectacular hosta a place in any garden. Journey's End grows to an imposing size with massive leaves in shades of green highlighted with brassy gold in sunshine. The stunning character and form, along with the wonderful pie-crust edge works well in sun or shade. The plant retains a more subtle attire in several shades of green in shade, highlighted in the center in gold and yellow in more sun.

H. *Dark Shadows*

The subtle beauty of this mysterious hosta often goes unnoticed as it sprawls in the shadows, streaked and feathered in deep blue-green just a shade or two darker than the surrounding leaf coloration. Dark Shadows is definitely a plant that deserves a closer look to fully appreciate its quiet, yet intense style.

In the sunshine, this effect this not as soft spoken as with plants located in shadier locations of the garden.

H. *Ebb Tide*

As if in perpetual motion, the long, richly elegant green and brassy gold foliage of Ebb Tide dances in the summer garden. Twisting and turning, often curling playfully at the leaf tip, the stunning vase-shaped architecture of this spectacular hosta is unmatched, each deeply veined leaf seemingly painted along the edges with shades of gold, olive and soft greens.

Over the years, the plant forms a massive mound of cascading leaves that tumble and fall over each other with shimmering grace.

H. *Beckoning*

Throughout the growing season, the beauty that is Beckoning transforms at a gentle pace each and every day.
Beginning the year dressed in a soft, understated green, the interior of the leaf transforms to a brassy white gold by summer's end,
light green to chartreuse in shade.
An offspring of the classic giant Blue Angel, Beckoning grows to become quite large in size, the perfect complement to other hosta
varieties in every color and size, as well as shade companions.

H. *Blueberry Ala Mode*

The world stopped spinning the second I first laid eyes upon a spectacular, mature specimen of Blueberry Ala Mode, in all its wrinkled, cupped, richly colorful splendor.

Massive, folded leaves, tremendously seer suckered or corrugated in deep blue, are feathered and frosted in creamy ivory, sprawling and stretching in all the plant's spectacular, unruly glory.

H. *Olive Branch*

As much as I love dramatic, vibrant variegation, I am perhaps more drawn to subtle graces of color and light that dress some of my favorite hosta gems. Olive Branch is one of these, with a center only marginally lighter and kissed with gold than its wide outer edge. The compact size and unusual coloration make this a wonderful addition to a border, container or shade garden, where it does well with just about any companion plant.

H. *Allegan Fog*

The hosta that started it all, Allegan Fog was my first must-have plant many years ago as I first dove into the world of hosta and discovered its classic, misted or spray-painted elegance on display at a local botanical garden. Transforming throughout the season from near white to heavily misted, silvery green with a wide, darker edge and playful undulation and twisting of its foliage, this remains one of my garden favorites.

H. *Pistache*

A fun and colorful plant in bright, pistachio green, with subtle touches of deeper green and blue, streaked and splattered with milky white, this beautiful sport of the classic Spilt Milk has taken its place among my favorite garden plants.

As it matures, the colorful leaves display a misted overlay of several shades of green and blue, with a distinct edge and the splattered milk pattern of its parent.

Like most hostas, Pistache grows better with age, each new season bringing a change in the character and texture of the plant, with an increase in corrugation, thickening of the leaves and size increase.

H. *Frosted Jade*

A mature specimen of this classic hosta makes an unbeatable specimen in the garden. Looking its best in full shade, the extravagant, elongated leaves, long stems and beautiful cascading form, frosted and feathered in beautiful white, truly packs a powerful punch. Stunning veining and just a tease of corrugation or seer suckering complete the graceful presence.

H. *Tattoo*

Another subtle beauty, with its transparent maple leaf pattern etched on leaves of chartreuse and gold, Tattoo is the nemesis plant of many hosta growers. With a reputation of being finicky and hard to grow to maturity, the challenge of nurturing a show stopping specimen earns this beauty a place among my favorites.

H. *Royal Tiara*

Unlike anything else out there, one of my "un-hostas", Royal Tiara is one of the most unique and interesting hosta varieties available. Hostas that don't look like hostas have always captivated me and this beauty with folded, curled and twisted leaves in bright green with a sparkling silver or white center resembles no other plant available.

Fun, colorful and outrageous, the elegance that is Royal Tiara deserves a place in every shade garden.

H. *Pandora's Box*

Among my favorites of the miniatures, Pandora's Box, with its tiny, children's teaspoon leaves streaked in bright white and deep green is a highly versatile and useful plant in gardens, containers and other displays. Paired with deeply colored miniatures such as Blue Mouse Ears or bizarre plants like Hacksaw or Corkscrew, this plant makes a breathtaking companion in a fun, compact miniature package.

H. *Mourning Dove*

For many seasons I admired the elegant form of Mourning Dove in repeated plantings in the rich shade gardens of a fellow hosta-adoring friend. It wasn't until relatively recently, when I was graced with the beauty of this graceful plant, drenched and shimmering in fresh morning rain, that I was prompted to pick up this fine specimen for my own ever-expanding hosta oasis.

H. *Lakeside Old Smokey*

Hostas of unusual coloration attract my eye and this beauty with stunning sea green hue, ghostly veining and unusual, rippled and slightly toothed edge is a winner. The soft, seafoam green coloration, with white underside and its beautiful growth form make this a wonderful specimen plant or companion to hosta varieties in rich blue, deep green or golden yellow.

H. Geisha

Fun and playful with curled leaves streaked and splattered in shades of green and gold, the spiraling leaves of this lively plant do wonderfully in beds, borders as well as in containers, where the stunning shape can be best appreciated. A wide edge in bright green surrounds the streaked and misted center. dressed in gold, flecked and dappled in shades of emerald.

H. *Hollywood Lights*

Beautiful and complex in coloration, Hollywood Lights shines in sun or shade. The intense coloration is best seen in full to part shade, where the subtle differences and multiple hues can be truly spectacular. In full, bright sun, these colors tend to wash out and lighter areas whiten. The grace and texture of this beautiful hosta make it a stunning garden centerpiece.

A CLOSER LOOK
STREAKED HOSTAS

The sweet dreams of many hosta breeders and growers are made of plants that feature ornate streaking or marbling. The rich effect of this type of foliage is highly sought after among breeders especially, who wish to pass on this form of variation to future seedlings.

Hostas with streaking, or marbling, on the leaves are available in many shapes, sizes and colors, from miniatures, such as those in the mouse ear family, to the most impressive of the giants.

Streaked hosta varieties are available in all colors. There are blue hosta, yellow, chartreuse, deeper green and near black forms available in streaked form. Many of these are held in the private gardens of those who bred them, to be used for future breeding endeavors down the road. Some, however, have been made commercially available.

The streaked effect has been produced in hostas of all shapes, sizes and textures as well. Some feature pointed, arrow-shaped leaves, some round, some are richly veined, some heavily seer-suckered.

The quest for the perfect "streaker" continues to inspire hosta breeders everywhere to fulfill their dreams each season as they watch seedlings mature into magnificent wonders of art.

Collecting streakers is a passion for many hosta growers, though it is easy for even beginner hosta gardeners to catch the craze. Beauties such as Korean Snow, Ice Age Trail, Vivacious, Savannah

Supreme, Galaxy, Christmas Tree Gala and others have become fairly easy to acquire.

Others may require some searching online and through specialty hosta retailers to add to your collection.

With each new season, untold numbers of new seedlings are produced that hold promise for future generations of hosta lovers. A vast number of these are prized streaked plants.

In addition to large, cascading types of hosta, my favorite streakers currently are those with gold or yellow foliage. There are surprisingly few varieties available in gold and yellow that feature this type of mottling or marbling.

Combined with an intense seer-suckering effect, cupped or folded leaves and outrageous unruliness, a large, messy, gold or yellow streaker would be a wonderful surprise.

Be cautious when including streaked or marbled hostas in your display beds. While they are fun and challenging to collect, the effect of a mass planting of streaked hostas in the garden tends to be overpowering. Too many streaked plants in one bed and they all tend to run together and look the same. This tends to downplay the beauty and elegance of their unusual foliage.

Streaked hostas make wonderful container plants, as well, especially those that feature cascading foliage or form a nice, sprawling specimen. These plants can be combined with annuals and perennials of all shapes and sizes for a wonderfully elegant container presentation.

An outstanding, unnamed seedling of Krossa Regal showing wonderfully streaked foliage.

Many a hosta breeder's dream! Corrugation, color and a breathtaking streaked and misted pattern dress this as yet unnamed hosta seedling.

H. *Emerald Ruff Cut*

I first fell in love with this plant while admiring its tranquil, cascading form and vase shape in the pages of a hosta reference guide. The plant certainly lives up to its name when seen in person, as it arches and flows gracefully with wonderfully decorated leaves awash in shades of green and gold, as well as its pristine, rippled edge.

Emerald Ruff Cut becomes even more breathtaking with age, as its leaves thicken and lengthen over the years, become even more intensely rippled at the edge and the plant begins to form a large and impressive clump.

H. *On Stage*

Sprawling in sun or shade, the massive leaves of On Stage impress and mesmerize those who pass by this outstanding plant in any garden. As beautiful in full sun as it is in deep shade, On Stage impresses with spectacular coloration, deep, rich veining, slight seersuckering and its large size.

Notoriously late in appearing in spring, On Stage quickly makes up for lost time by unfurling its colorful golden leaves, edged and feathered in shades of bright green, gradually transforming to near-white by midsummer.

H. *Sum and Substance*

Among of the biggest and the best, this excellent, versatile, colorful plant with its massive, rubbery leaves in beautiful chartreuse, brightening to gleaming yellow in full sun, remains one of my favorites. Fast growing, bright and beautiful, Sum and Substance is the parent plant of a large number of equally magnificent offspring. Excellent in full sun or full shade, this is among the most versatile of all hosta varieties available.

H. *Lakeside Paisley Print*

Impossibly beautiful in several shades of green with flashy feathering in chartreuse, gold and white, nothing matches the breathtaking beauty of a mature specimen of Lakeside Paisley Print in the garden. Incredibly ornate ripples along the leaf edge add to the stunning and pristine elegance of this wonderful medium-sized hosta, one like no other on the market.

For the best coloration and pattern, grow this plant in full to part shade. Fuller sun tends to wash out and fade the subtle shades that dance and swirl at the leaf center.

H. *June*

Still topping popularity polls everywhere, hosta lovers bow to the queen. Elegant, colorful, tough, versatile and nearly indestructible, this is a powerhouse plant that only grows better with time.

Extremely vigorous and versatile, June grows equally well in full shade or full sun.

Depending upon location, the plant may be richly painted in blues and greens in shady spots, or boast more striking and dramatic variegation in white and deep green with more sun.

H. *Linda Sue*

With a dramatic, wide leaf edge in beautiful gold surrounding a deeper green center flare, the massive, leathery leaves of Linda Sue sprawl in beautiful form upon tall, thick stems.

This plant will do well in sun where its lighter edge is less susceptible to burning than similar hosta varieties that tend to brown or melt along the leaf border.

As it matures into a magnificent specimen, Linda Sue becomes a stunning addition to the hosta garden, especially alongside hosta varieties in shades of blue and gold.

H. *Montana Aureomarginata*

With dramatic coloration and elegant, vase shape, Montana Aureomarginata is a stunner. Its long, richly veined, slightly pointed leaves in beautiful gold and green, fading to white in sun, explode outward in breathtaking form, cascading in elegant fashion to drape like a stunning gown.

One of the classic large to giant hostas, Montana Aureomarginata grows slowly to full maturity, a journey of patience that is rewarded with a showcase specimen in the garden.

H. *Sunshine Glory*

Glory, to be sure, this spectacular hosta in bright, gleaming yellow when placed in full sun, sparkles with a crisp, snow-white edge. Heavy corrugation and an upright growth habit makes this prized hosta a classic, bright and fanciful beauty. Place in full to part sun for the most intense yellow coloration. The leaves will remain a bright green or chartreuse with more shade.

H. *Bridal Falls*

An exciting, variegated form of the classic Niagara Falls, Bridal Falls features the same stunning green leaves, intense rippled edge and vase-shaped form of its parent plant with a beautiful and elegant edge in brilliant white.

Like most hosta varieties, this plant only improves with age and maturity as the coloration, margin width and piecrust edge become more prominent over the years.

TEXTURE TEMPTATIONS

Much of the beauty of hostas in the garden resides in the wonderful, elegant textures that dance across the leaf surfaces. Hostas are masterpieces of texture in the garden, featuring any number of wonderfully rich textures that serve to draw interest, catch the eye and frolic with other plants in the garden.

Some hosta varieties feature a wonderful corrugation or seer-suckered effect, growing more intense and defined with age. Other plants feature deep, attractive veining or ribbing along both surfaces of the leaf, making them just as beautiful and elegant from above as below. There are also hostas which feature a smooth, polished look, sometimes opaque in appearance, other times shimmering and glossy.

With texture comes the wonderfully elegant piecrust edge present in many wonderful forms, some with loose waves, others quite intensely rippled.

With certain magnificent specimens, you get a combination of all of these magnificent features, resulting in one truly magnificent standout plant in the garden.

Hostas such as Queen of the Seas, Manhattan, Fluted Fountain, Lakeside Full Tide and others feature all of these wonderful characteristics on one plant.

Unruly hostas that feature heavy corrugation as well as deep cupping of the leaves are among my favorites. These include plants such as Abiqua Drinking Gourd, World Cup, Love Pat, Neat and Tidy, Black Hills and many others.

When planning your garden beds, consider texture as one of your key design elements. Combining richly textured hostas with other perennials that feature wonderful textures themselves, unusual or classic growth forms and leaf shapes helps to create an even more intricate and richly elegant display.

H. *High Society*

While this plant has a reputation of being somewhat touchy, High Society remains one of my favorite June sports with intense coloration in shades of blue, green and white, toughness and long-lasting beauty.

Like June and Remember Me, High Society will fade to near white with more sun. I prefer giving it ample shade where its true colors and complex, brush-stroke pattern in several shades will truly shine.

H. *Gunther's Prize*

Quite possibly the king of all hosta to many, this highly prized treasure with its complex and variable streaking and splattering of emerald green over a bright chartreuse or yellow background, is truly spectacular. Gunther's Prize, like its parent plant, Sum and Substance, grows to immense size, gleaming even brighter in full sun.

Its unique and unusual variegation and streaking make it a treasured giant among the world of hosta.

H. *Halcyon*

Elegant and stunning in soft, rich, silvery blue, Halcyon is the parent plant of many of our finest hosta specialties. Its characteristic form, colorful leaves, thick, rubbery substance and amazing versatility make it one of the most useful hosta varieties in design and containers.

For the richest blue, place the plant in mostly shade. The blue bloom will fade to a rich, glossy dark green in brighter sun.

H. *Sun Kissed*

Like beautiful stained glass, morning sun shimmering through the densely corrugated, bright green leaves of Sun Kissed sparkles like gleaming gems in the garden. A medium sized hosta, the full, rounded leaves, feathered and tipped in pure white, are colored an unusual shade of brilliant yellow-green, even more brilliant with some sun. The leaves are often held upright, giving the plant a unique, glittering effect.

H. *Cold Heart*

Another of my favorite unusual hosta varieties, the beauty and wonder of Cold Heart displays itself in its heavily corrugated, beautifully rippled, unusually colored leaves in subtle yellow-green. The corrugation really becomes prominent as the plant matures, becoming almost unruly on aged plants. The character of Cold Heart is among my top favorites each season.

H. *Golden Meadows*

A stunning masterpiece in texture, character, architecture and color, Golden Meadows is a treasure among hosta varieties, growing to immense proportions as it transforms from day to day, week to week throughout the growing season. Crimped and folded edges in deep blue green surround a feathery, streaked interior that begins the season near-white, becoming flecked and misted in deeper bluish green as the weeks go by.

The large, leathery leaves, brilliantly colored and formed throughout the season, fold, curl and twist elegantly, overlapping into a large, mostly upright clump that truly impresses.

H. *Moonlight Sonata*

Shimmering like opaque glass in the deepest shadows of the shade garden, the full, rounded leaves of Moonlight Sonata glisten in the dappled sunlight. Smooth, polished leaves reflect moonlight in the evening, creating a stunning effect in the garden after dark. Colored a beautiful, rich bluish green with teal highlights, Moonlight Sonata is a treasured gem among hosta lovers.

H. *Gentle Giant*

Truly living up to its name, the gentle, towering stems of Gentle Giant hold loosely folded, cupped leaves in soft, gentle blue green. Forming a massive clump of nearly upright foliage that loosely waves downward at the edge, Gentle Giant is a graceful, subtle behemoth that stands well on its own or surrounded by smaller, colorful hosta and other shade plants at its massive feet.

H. *Sir Richard*

A showstopper in the garden, the stunning and elegant piecrust edge, pointed leaves and beautifully streaked foliage in green, gold and a hint of blue make Sir Richard a highly sought after addition. The parent plant of both The King and The Queen, Sir Richard features the same beautiful, rippled edge, only with breathtaking marbled and streaked leaves.

RIPPLES ARE ALL THE RAGE

An elegant trend in hosta breeding is producing plants with even more extravagant ruffling and rippling along the leaf edge, sometimes extending all the way down the stem to the crown. Hostas with this type of edge add a playfulness and elegance to the garden, seemingly in constant motion, waving, fluttering, flowing with the summer breeze.

From loose, undulating waves to intense piecrust edges, hostas with rippled margins are hot among growers of these amazing plants. The ripple effect can present itself in many ways. On some plants, it is a fun, lively, outlandish look. On other plants, the effect is pure elegance, grace and class.

Combined with other attractive attributes and characteristics such as intense corrugation, pointed leaves, twisting, curling and, of course, coloration, rippled margins help to produce a spectacular specimen.

Often, the rippling and piecrust edge comes with age. Young plants often display only a hint, if any clue at all, to what's to come in several growing seasons.

The true masterpieces may take as long as 5 to 7 years to display their fully mature characteristics. Others may need a somewhat shorter timeframe, requiring only 3 to 4 growing seasons.

The wait is worth it when it comes to relishing the treasured form and beauty of a properly nurtured specimen in the garden.

H. Shimmy Shake is an example of a hosta that features an elegant ruffled or rippled leaf edge.
Some other hostas available with rippled or piecrust edges include Lakeside Full Tide, Lakeside Surf Rider,
Queen of the Seas, Komodo Dragon, Niagara Falls, Bridal Falls, War Paint, Curly Fries, Ripple Effect,
Lakeside Old Smokey, Dancing Queen, Lakeside Paisley Print, Whee, The King and Manhattan.

H. *Foxfire Palm Sunday*

Unlike any other hosta, the spectacular, octopus-like foliage of Foxfire Palm Sunday sprawls beautifully in the shade. An interesting, deeper green pattern brushed with feathered or palm-like appearance shadows the center of each elongated leaf.

This plant becomes better with age as it leaves continue to lengthen, the central variegation becomes more pronounced and the chartreuse to gold edge widens. An all-gold sport, Foxfire Good Friday is equally unusual and stunning.

H. *Celebration of Angels*

Unruliness among hostas is one of my favorite characteristics of these plants and this big, brassy, mess of a beauty does not disappoint. In beautiful, crinkled and corrugated bright yellow, Celebration of Angels in a sunny location is a truly breathtaking sight.

Pair it with smaller hosta varieties in rich blue, as well as other colorful perennials and foliage plants for a wonderful, easy and unusual plant combination, complete with incredible texture, fun and interesting form and long-lasting beauty.

H. *Lakeside Prophecy*

Another plant I instantly fell for upon first sight, this near-black beauty boasts perhaps the most intense, heavy corrugation of any hosta. Thick, leathery leaves are nearly completely covered in richly textured seer-suckering, along with an elegant, rippled edge at maturity.

The near-black color complements lighter colored hosta and companion plants beautifully.

H. *Regalia*

The subtle, understated beauty of this regal plant often goes unnoticed in the garden unless the observer pauses to take a closer look. Muted shades of soft blue, green and several shades in between come together to dress each leaf in elegant, soft-spoken grace. The towering, vase shape comes courtesy of its parent plant, Krossa Regal.

H. *Mango Tango*

Bright and bouncy, the deliciousness of this tropical-looking beauty is refreshing in the summer garden. Lush leaves in bright green with a slightly crimped, folded center in beautiful gold appear to dance and sing during the height of summer.

H. *Mary Marie Ann*

The twisted and gracefully curved leaves of this wonderful hosta feature contrasting variegation in deep gray-green and white or chartreuse, depending on the amount of sunshine provided. The plant features a crimped or embroidered edge, similar to Golden Meadows, along with leaves that undulate beautifully and twist at the tips.

H. *Hyuga Urajiro*

With extremely long, streaked leaves in several shades of green and blue, this wonderful specimen plant is another beauty that many gardeners would never guess is a hosta. The plant also features wonderfully elegant and unusual flowers that burst from thin flowering stems like summer fireworks.

H. *Mountain Snow*

Gracing the shadows with beautiful leaves in deep green and painted feathers of chalky white that frolic among the leaf tips and edges, Mountain Snow unfurls like a breath of fresh air in the deep shadows. Its large size and beautifully painted, overlapping leaves form a spectacular showpiece in the summer garden.

H. *The King*

Another hosta that many growers either love or hate due to its touchier nature and tendency to drawstring at the edge. The King is an elegant and beautiful plant with feathery brass edge surrounding a richer, green center. An elegantly rippled edge creates a wonderful effect as it waves from the shadows.

H. *Goodness Gracious*

Growing more spectacular with each passing season, this hosta, with wide gold edge, narrow, deeper green leaf center and wonderfully piecrusted edge offers a spectacular presentation. Dramatic and distinctive leaf veining adds to the beauty of this stunning hosta that holds its leaves horizontally in a magnificent display.

H. *Stargate*

When I first saw this towering beauty in the garden of Jennifer Peterson, Menasha, Wisconsin, I was hooked. Its impressive, vertical stance and shimmering glossy leaf substance, inherited from parent Flower Power, as well as an intensely streaked and misted center, set this one apart. The leaves are often held horizontally from the stem creating a wonderful effect from this vase-shaped beauty.

A SEA OF COLOR

A sprawling sea of turquoise, blue and green dances before me as my eyes rise and fall with the waves of serene hostas that flow like water, glimmering in the dappled sunlight that sparkles through the treetops. The calming colors of hostas make them a wonderful choice for gardeners who aim to escape into their private oases.

In endless shades of blue and green, with whitecaps that flash and frolic among the undulating mounds, a garden of hostas soothes and relieves, if only in its tranquil color combinations.

The colors of hosta are varied and rich. Some look their best in full shade, while others are best showcased in brilliant sun. In some cases, the same plant may look completely different in sun and shade, making these choices even more valuable and versatile. Hosta June is a prime example.

For some hosta growers, shades of blue are favored. Hosta varieties come in all shades of blue, from light gray to deep, rich, midnight blue. Sky blue, turquoise and aquamarine are among my favorites. Many of the blues look their best in shade, tending to transform to shades of green or gray with more sun.

Yellow, chartreuse or gold hosta selections offer spectacular shimmering beauty wherever they are mixed in among the deeper shades of blue and green.

Of course, there are hostas in every shade of green imaginable, from the lightest sea foam to near-black.

Variegated and streaked hostas mix and match coloration with spectacular results. Some plants feature leaves brushed, streaked or marbled with multiple shades of green, blue, gold, white and more.

The coloration of hostas can be used to create masterpieces of art in the garden. Combining and designing with hostas of different colors is a great way to showcase your favorite plants and bring out the best in each plant included in these combinations.

A great way to combine hosta varieties is to select plants in colors that are reflected in each other. For example, the glowing chartreuse of the leaf interior of H. Gypsy Rose is reflected in the solid coloration of stunning H. Prairie Moon. Planted side by side, each plant is elevated by the pairing.

Companion plants, including annuals, perennials, bulbs, trees and shrubs can all be used to accent or reflect hosta colors and patterns as well. Use contrasting colors to truly highlight a favorite hosta. Bright orange lilies planted among a sea of rich blue hosta creates a striking display.

Think beyond leaf color when considering planting options, as well. Many hosta varieties feature striking "legs" in rich reds and purples that make quite an impact when planted in raised beds or containers.

H. *Queen of the Seas*

I'm still longing for the moment when Queen of the Seas is honored as Hosta of the Year. If ever a plant was so deserving, this is the one. Stunning in maturity with heavily corrugated, deeply veined leaves with gorgeous piecrust edges, brushed in a rich aqua blue, Queen of the Seas is one spectacular selection.

H. *Spilt Milk*

The classic streaked and mottled beauty in an unusual shade of bluish green with variable "milk splatter" highlights, Spilt Milk remains one of my favorites, a classic that deserves a place in any hosta grower's garden. A thick leaf substance, elegant blooms, unusual foliage and a dramatic form at maturity make this plant a breathtaking specimen.

H. *Hanky Panky*

One of many striking sports of the classic hosta Striptease, Hanky Panky undergoes a fascinating seasonal transformation. Colorful and dramatic in the spring as it emerges in bright whitish-gold or yellow with a richer green central leaf, the colors change frequently throughout the season. Given more sun, the coloration and pattern becomes even more breathtaking.

H. *Manhattan*

Another odd, unruly and massive beauty, Manhattan combines a rich, emerald green color with intense seer-suckering or pebbling, along with a dramatic frilled and ruffled edge. This beauty is pretty in pink during spring as its newly emerged shoots are colored in rich rosy pink, as are the flower buds and stems later in the season.

H. *Abiqua Drinking Gourd*

With massive, cupped leaves that are heavily corrugated and rubbery in substance at maturity, Abiqua Drinking Gourd is an imposing and show-stopping plant in the garden. This plant takes several years to reach maturity, which, unfortunately, works to the plants disadvantage. Gardeners who visit their local garden centers likely pass this plant by on the growing tables as its unimpressive first and second-year appearance doesn't draw the eye. Patience is required to nurture a mighty specimen.

H. *Great Expectations*

Love it or hate it, that's the theme among hosta growers on this beautiful plant. One of several varieties that have a reputation of being finicky, Great Expectations, when happy, is among the most striking and beautiful of all hosta varieties. Painted in beautiful layers of rich blue, shades of green, gold and white, Great Expectations, especially when grown in shade, is an elegant beauty.

H. *Lakeside Butterball*

Dressed in the most beautiful shade of soft, buttery yellow, slightly brighter in sun, Lakeside Butterball is a perfectly-named selection. Unfortunately, this breathtaking plant is also becoming quite hard to find. Large, rounded, smooth leaves touched with only slight corrugation sprawl in a rather low-growing, horizontal mound that truly shows off the unusual and stunning coloration.

INTO THE LIGHT

Out of the shadows and into the light, hosta growers are discovering more and more varieties that do quite well even with a full day of sunshine. Some of the best hosta growers have discovered that many plants grow better in the sun, where they see quicker, more accelerated growth, albeit somewhat smaller leaf size.

Hostas that do well in sun range across the board in plant characteristics and traits. Therefore, there is no easy way to define hostas that do well in sun. For example, very generally, most thinner-leaved varieties do better in shade. However, there are many wonderful hostas that defy this generalization and grow excellent in even full, hot sun.

Most blues tend to do better in full to part shade, while yellows perform wonderfully overall in sun. Many variegated hostas will do fine in sun. However, the downside is that you lose some of the complex variegation and hidden, subtle brushstrokes of color that are apparent when grown in more shade. In sun, this variegation tends to fade to simple green and white, which, in itself provides wonderful contrast and a striking appearance.

Many hosta breeders agree that some sun is best to showcase "streakers."

Some examples of excellent hosta choices for sun include Sum and Substance, Winter Snow, Paul's Glory, Liberty, Sun Power, Paradigm, Gunther's Prize, Sunshine Glory, Lakeside Cha Cha, June, Guacamole, Golden Tiara, Stained Glass, Cathedral Windows, Solar Flare, Dream Queen, Fragrant Bouquet and many others.

H. *Winter Lightning*

With an addicting beauty, this plant has foiled me many times. I include it here among my favorites, not because it is easy to grow or find, but precisely because of the challenge in maintaining a beautiful and pristine specimen. Several times, I have purchased the plant, only to have it revert to a solid green within a season or two. Yet, its tantalizing beauty and unique coloration and pattern are too tempting. Quite a stunner, indeed.

H. *Rainbow's End*

Grown in full shade, Rainbow's End is one of the most beautifully colored and patterned hosta varieties available. Its striking pattern, brush-stroked in deep green, yellow, white, and several shades of green in between, make this bright and colorful plant an obvious winner. With more sun, the variegation tends to fade to standard green and white, therefore, placing in appropriate shade will help maintain the beautiful, complex coloration.

H. *Whee*

For fun in the shade, nothing beats the curly, twisted, rippled leaves and stems of this delightful small to medium-sized plant. In constant motion, it appears, the leaves spiral and radiate from the crown, curling and overlapping in wonderful joyous abandon.

H. *Dream Queen*

With massive, lily pad leaves that are almost leathery to the touch, beautiful and striking Dream Queen is a plant that, like many hosta varieties, gets better with age. As the plant matures, the central flare of creamy yellow narrows as the thick, deep blue-green edge widens. With just a lightning strike of color in the leaf center and slight feathering, the effect is truly marvelous. Holds it beautiful yellow central color best in shade.

H. *Roy Klehm*

A fascinating hosta, subtly dressed in several shades of bright green that maintain just enough distinction to create a unusual and stunning pattern. This is a medium to large hosta that looks its best in mostly shade.

H. *Guardian Angel*

Blessed in blue, silver, green and gray, Guardian Angel is my favorite among all of the hosta varieties of the world. An inspiring, looming and captivating specimen, with its misted center in blue-green and silver and feathered edge in deeper blue and green, Guardian Angel is another hosta that transforms week by week throughout the growing season. In the spring, the center of the leaf is nearly white, gradually acquiring a gentle mist of blue-green throughout spring and summer. Not as fast-growing as its parent, Blue Angel, nevertheless this plant is a must-have addition to any hosta display.

H. *London Fog*

Dazzling in flecked minty green, this sport of Allegan Fog carries its parent's misted center throughout the entire leaf surface, losing the deeper green, solid edge and much of the fanciful curling effect. Somewhat slow to start, London Fog forms a beautiful and unusual clump of elongated leaves after several growing seasons.

H. *Dust Devil*

Subtlety at its finest, the unusually colored margins and interior of this Whirlwind offspring boasts shades of green not commonly seen among fellow hosta varieties. A rich, lovely deep olive surrounds an even darker center overlaid with narrow ribbons of silver and a hint of bluish-green. In order for the hosta to display of these rich colors, keep the plant in full to part shade. Sunlight will wash out the richest coloration and overlapping layers.

H. *Praying Hands*

Still in a class all its own, this wonderfully unique and unusual plant, with its upright, vertical, folded leaves, heavy ribbing and thick substance, is a prized specimen. With a beautiful and lively upright growth habit, Praying Hands makes a wonderful container plant, where the unusual form can be proudly displayed and appreciated.

H. *Parhelion*

Another of the magnificent sports of giant Sum and Substance, Parhelion brings a slightly different shade of green, a slight matte finish to the leaves and a variable, pencil-thin white edge that truly makes a mark all its own. In rich, beautiful, bright green, Parhelion lights up the shadows, glowing in a widespread and elegant mass of vibrant color in even the deepest shade.

H. *Midnight at the Oasis*

Beautiful and ominous, the deep dark leaves of a mature specimen late in the summer create a sense of mystery in the garden. The leaves emerge nearly white with a deep dark edge in the spring, gradually darkening in the center throughout the growing season as an eerie mist flecks each upright leaf.

MATTERS OF SIZE

For many passionate hosta growers, it all comes down to a matter of size when it comes to seeking out and nurturing incredible hostas to maturity. These garden stalwarts grow to become some of the largest plants available to gardeners. In fact, many varieties grow to five or 6 feet across at maturity, even larger in some cases. Some of these may boast leaves of 18 inches in length and almost as wide.

At the opposite end of the spectrum are tiny miniatures that may reach only 6 inches wide with leaves barely the size of your fingernail.

Hosta connoisseurs have many different tastes in plants. Some prefer the sprawling, dominating behemoths that loom in the shadows with a solid beauty, while others are fond of miniatures that are perfect for planters, containers, rock gardens and borders.

Depending upon who you talk to you, there may be anywhere from 3 to 6 or more size classifications used to distinguish hostas. These are not always accurate as some hostas classified as small could easily exceed the dimensions of a medium or large plant if left undisturbed long enough in the garden.

General classifications of miniature, small, medium, large and giant seem to work best.

Miniature hostas include those tiny wonders in the mouse ear family, as well as beauties like Pandora's Box and Cameo.

Small hostas might include plants such as June, Curly Fries, Tattoo, Hacksaw and Golden Tiara.

Medium-sized plants such as Striptease, Lakeside Paisley Print, Whirlwind, The King, Bridegroom and Deep Blue Sea, work great as filler plants and in borders and containers.

Large hostas, such as Guardian Angel, Dream Queen, Gold Standard, Paradigm, Jewel of the Nile, Rascal, Love Pat and others serve as great anchors for garden beds or as stand-alone specimens.

True giants, such as Sum and Substance, Empress Wu, Climax, Solar Flare, Blue Angel, Mr. Big, Big Daddy, Celestial and others make wonderful mature specimen hostas in the garden that serve as breathtaking centerpiece plants.

H. *Foxfire Off Limits*

Bright, beautiful, lively and quite unusual, this plant features banana yellow leaves in summer with a slightly deeper wash of bright green along the edge. This plant does well in the sun, where this gold color becomes even brassier. Long, pointed leaves are held outward in parallel layers, creating a beautiful effect in garden beds and borders.

H. *Lakeside Looking Glass*

In full shade, the incredible, glossy beauty of this unusual plant is best displayed. Transparent veins glow in soft silver against the deep, blackish green leaves, polished to perfection in a wonderful sheen.

Short stems carry the loosely undulating leaves to form a low-growing mound that, despite its near black color, positively shines even in the darkest shadows.

H. *Fallen Angel*

Smoky gray-green in color, with an ornate, loose, piecrust edge, Fallen Angel boasts large leaves wholly misted, flecked and overlaid with a layer of bluish green. A sport of the classic Guardian Angel, Fallen Angel is a bizarre and unusual specimen, quite unlike any other hosta.

H. *Neat and Tidy*

Anything but, Neat and Tidy is one of those monstrous, unruly masses of a plant that I adore so deeply. Large and richly colored in forest green, the round, lily pad leaves crumple, fold, wrinkle, pebble and overlap to create one big beautiful mess.

H. *Summer Breeze*

One of the most beautifully named hostas, this plant billows like its namesake summer wind, awash in a beautiful combination of yellow and green, fading to brassy gold or white along the wide edge with more sun. As the plant matures, gentle seer-suckering becomes more evident and the leaves begin to form a beautiful medium-sized clump of cheerful, colorful foliage.

H. *Fire Island*

One of the classic yellows, featuring beautiful red stems, Fire Island is a wonderful plant to display in containers and raised beds where this effect can be best appreciated. When grown in more sun, Fire Island retains more of its brilliant, yellow color. With more shade, the shimmering brilliance transforms to a more subtle, chartreuse during the growing season.

H. *Touch of Class*

At the top of my list as I began collecting hostas, Touch of Class used to be quite difficult to find. This elegant, classy sport of June features a thin stripe of chartreuse to silvery green surrounded by a wide, rich blue edge. Tough and durable and versatile in the garden, I prefer to grow Touch of Class in the shade where its beautiful blue and green coloration is at its finest. With more sun, the center of the leaf fades to cream or white, while the edge transforms to a darker green.

H. *Rainforest Sunrise*

This lively sprite of a hosta shimmers and sparkles in full sun as its puckered, seer-suckered leaves in bright lime green with gold highlights are kissed by the summer sun. A beautiful edge in sparkling emerald surrounds each round leaf, creating a wonderful display of brilliance and brightness in the summer garden.

H. *Korean Snow*

This medium sized, high-gloss, streaked hosta does well in sun or shade, displaying its muted, subtle, marbled effect wonderfully.

While its thin leaves are a drawback to some, the sparkling beauty of Korean Snow in the garden is something I treasure and look forward to seeing every year.

H. *El Niño*

Among the many hosta varieties of similar coloration and pattern, El Niño tends to be my favorite due to its steadfast color in beautiful turquoise, crisp white edge and elegant, delicate ruffling at the leaf edge.

H. *Dorothy Benedict*

The mother of many spectacular variegated and streaked hostas, Dorothy Benedict is a prized plant for many hosta collectors and breeders. Because of its rare beauty, this plant still commands a high price in the marketplace. Elegant, wonderfully textured, beautifully feathered and marbled in cream, gold, green and blue, Dorothy Benedict is one amazing and beloved hosta.

SEASONAL TRANSFORMATIONS

Among my favorite hosta varieties are those that undergo seasonal transformations that completely change the plant appearance from spring through the end of the growing season. Many wonderful hostas are well known for the characteristic, chameleon-like color changes they exhibit throughout the year.

Some may gradually transform from lighter colors to dark, while others undergo the opposite transformation.

I am especially fond of those hostas that undergo their transformation with an elegant spray-painted or misted appearance. Plants like Golden Meadows, Guardian Angel, Allegan Fog and others emerge nearly pure white or ivory color in the interior of the leaf. As the weeks go by, a spray-painted or misted appearance begins to appear, flecking the leaf in richer, darker bluish-green. By the end of the growing season, some of these plants may be solid green in color once this gradual transformation is complete.

Classic hosta Beckoning undergoes the opposite transformation. The leaves of this large sport of Blue Angel emerge a solid, bluish green color, gradually whitening throughout the growing season. By midsummer, the massive leaves are colored a beautiful white-gold or chartreuse, depending on light conditions, with a thin, deeper green edge.

To watch these beauties undergo this magical transformation throughout the season brings a whole new level of passion to growing and enjoying hosta.

H. Hanky Panky is another well-known chameleon among hostas. Fresh leaves emerge rich gold and yellow with a bright green center, transforming to several subtle shades of green by summer's end.

H. Golden Meadows in spring features central coloration that is mostly white or ivory.

By mid-summer, the leaf center of H. Golden Meadows has undergone a beautiful transformation, with a spray-painted or misted wash of blue-green that continues to deepen throughout the rest of the season.

HOSTAS OF THE FUTURE

The world of hostas continues to grow ever brighter as top breeders throughout the world strive to pursue their passions, creating wonderful new hybrids, as well as developing plant characteristics, traits, patterns, colors and other surprises many of us have long dreamed of.

Streaked hostas, of course, tend to be among the most popular when it comes to breeding. And there are many fine, new streaked varieties available each season.

Hosta breeders continue to explore leaf color, with red, purples and blues taking precedence. Many hosta varieties have been introduced with red stems and petioles that blush onto the leaf surface. This trend continues to expand this coloration deeper and deeper into the leaf.

Recently, H. First Blush, the first widely available red-leaved hosta, hit the marketplace, causing quite a sensation. It will be interesting to see what becomes of this plant, as well as others vying for similar glory.

The world of hostas recently enjoyed another surprise in the form of H. Miracle Lemony, a hosta with wonderful, lemon yellow blooms. Flower color is another area hosta hybridizers are exploring. Hostas with pink, blue and yellow blooms are out there. Can red, orange or deep violet be far behind?

Unusual forms are also intriguing to hosta breeders. Elongated leaves, twists, curls and unruliness are all the rage. Hostas that look nothing like hostas continue to impress.

Of course, there are those who continue to breed for sheer size. Many impressive varieties continue to be unveiled each season that eventually promise to form immense clumps that will dominate the garden.

Bold patterns and coloration are always popular among hosta lovers and equally popular are more subtle surprises such as tattoos, watermarks and mists or streaking that shimmer on the leaf surface.

H. Infatuation features deeply colored stems that bleed onto the leaf surface.

H. *Kiwi Full Monty*

The classic Striptease sport in beautiful powder blue, Kiwi Full Monty has become one of the most popular hosta varieties available. The plant retains more of its blue shine when planted in the shade. Here, the subtle differences between the central portion and outer edge, in addition to the thin white lightning stripes that separate the two, are at their best. A beautiful, rich teal to aquamarine in spring, Kiwi Full Monty is pure heaven and joy in the garden.

H. *St. Elmo's Fire*

Rising from the soil cloaked in rich red leggings, the flaming gold of St. Elmo's Fire burns in the spring landscape. With leaf edges fringed in bright white, the raging colors of this wonderful plant flame throughout the seasons. St. Elmo's Fire does well in full sun where its bright foliage gleams a joyful lemon yellow throughout summer and into fall.

H. *Delta Pride*

One of just a handful of yellow streakers, Delta Pride, with its extravagant seer-suckering, brushstroke marbling in lighter shades of yellow, ivory and cream and large growth habit, creates a spectacular and unusual garden specimen. In the shade, the leaves take on a more chartreuse to lime green hue, brighter and brassier with sun. A fun, bold and striking hosta.

H. *Brother Stefan*

Tough, rugged and exceptionally beautiful, the extreme seer-suckering, leathery leaves and wonderful, widespread growth habit of this plant dominate the garden wherever it is put on display. Brother Stefan will tolerate some sun, where its coloration will fade somewhat. Young plants take a few seasons to develop the heavy corrugation that comes with maturity.

H. *Earth Angel*

An elegant and subtle beauty in creamy ivory, silver and several shades of green, Earth Angel is a stunning sport of the classic giant Blue Angel. Young plants for sale at garden centers do not do the mature splendor of this plant justice. It takes several years for the plant to reach full size and develop the spectacular streaking, feathering and painted appearance the mature beauty is prized for.

H. *Climax*

One of the spectacular giants, Climax has so much to offer. Beautiful coloration in shades of green and gold, heavy corrugation or seer-suckering, immense size and long-lasting beauty in the garden, this is a powerhouse plant, guaranteed to impress visitors to the garden.

H. *Confused Angel*

A complex, streaked sport of Blue Angel, Confused Angel is brushed and marbled with shades of ivory, gold, blue, green and silver, arrayed over the entire leaf surface, resulting in a spectacular display in the garden. The coloration is best defined in full to part shade, where the many different hues and patterns remain distinct and separate as they dance over the sprawling mound of breathtaking foliage.

H. *Montana Chirifu*

A hard-to-find, elegant beauty, this sweeping masterpiece in rich green with streaked and flecked foliage in snowy silver has grown to become one of my favorites. The delicate gleam of diamond dust across the beautifully painted leaf surface is at its best in spring, slowly fading to a more consistent green throughout the season.

H. *Filagree*

With unusually splattered and streaked leaves in shades of green and gold, Filagree is a one-of-a-kind specimen. Unfortunately, many growers are frightened off, mistakenly believing this plant contains the hosta virus X. Its appearance certainly is similar to plants infected by this disease, however, consistent testing has shown the plants to be healthy. The coloration is at its best in spring, dramatic and colorful. Throughout the growing season, the overall leaf color transforms to a solid, deep green.

H. *Ice Age Trail*

A classic, gorgeous streaked hosta, Ice Age Trail, with its heavy corrugation, creamy streaking throughout the leaf surface and relatively compact size make it a wonderful specimen for borders, containers and gardens. Streaking is variable on each plant, with some leaves displaying impressive variegation, while others may be nearly solid colored in green or blue.

H. *Liberty*

In garden centers, Liberty looks no different than any other variegated green and white plant. However, given four or five years in its place in the garden, this massive, elegant, striking hosta truly becomes one on its own. With tremendous, creamy white edges, richly feathered and streaked into a deeper green center, Liberty presents a stunning display in the garden.

H. *World Cup*

One of only a few yellow cupped hosta varieties, World Cup is rapidly becoming one of my favorites as it matures in my garden. Heavily seer-suckered, elegantly cupped leaves grow large and strong, almost leathery to the touch. The beautiful, bright chartreuse coloration transforms to rich, golden yellow with more sun. Stunning in form, World Cup stands proudly upright, towering over its neighbors and companions.

H. *Eye Declare*

An example of a hosta that should be much more popular and widely available than it is, Eye Declare is one of the most beautiful and brilliantly colored plants of medium to large size that brightens any area it graces. Emerging a beautiful, bright chartreuse or yellow-green with a thin wire edge in deeper emerald, the plant grows even brighter with sun throughout the season.

H. *Lakeside Reflecting Glass*

Smooth and glossy, marbled in creamy white and yellow over darker green, this is the streaked sport of Lakeside Looking Glass. The plant grows low and relatively wide, creating a beautiful look in the garden. Undulating edges dance in the shadows to create a burst of radiating beauty. Lakeside Reflecting Glass only becomes better with age as its leaves thicken and the pattern becomes even more variable and unpredictable.

H. *Sun Power*

Another classic giant, loosely rippled leaves in brilliant yellow sprawl in the summer sun, richly veined and elegantly poised. Sun Power remains one of my favorites due to its stunning leaf texture, large size and ability to stand on its own wherever planted. In sun or shade, the plant remains spectacular.

H. *Paradise Power*

A striking sport of Sun Power with a distinct, thin edge in shades of deeper green, Paradise Power proudly shows off its long, undulating leaves and beautiful texture throughout the year. I like this plant in more shade where the contrast of chartreuse and forest green, with just a kiss of blue, is particularly wonderful.

H. *Regal Splendor*

Tall, flowing waves of blue and ivory dance and tower over most other hosta in the garden when Regal Splendor reaches maturity. A sport of Krossa Regal with a thin, creamy edge, this plant forms a massive, vase-shaped tower of loosely ruffled leaves, colored beautiful turquoise in full shade, deeper green with more sun.

H. *Pizzazz*

In elegant feathered cream over a beautiful slate blue, Pizzazz took a while to grow on me as it is slow to mature. When age and maturity set in, the plant suddenly stands apart from so many other similarly patterned varieties. The leaves are held slightly upright, of an unusual, rounded shape, with extravagant feathering of cream at the tips and edges. Moderate corrugation or seer-suckering completes the beautiful effect and the sprawling array of foliage seems to dance among the shadows.

H. *Barbara Ann*

A lesser known but striking beauty, Barbara Ann is a medium to large, heavily corrugated plant in beautiful, deep green with one of the brightest and most elegant white edges I've ever seen. An incredible specimen, the striking contrast between the brilliant, clear white and deep green is stunning in the summer garden. The heavy leaf texture, along with beautiful coloration, is quite outstanding, even with such a large number of similarly patterned hosta varieties.

H. *Nigrescens*

One of the most beautiful hosta available in terms of architecture and form, the slightly cupped leaves and tall, vertical stems offer a fabulous presentation. The soft, gray-green coloration adds even more beauty to this fantastic specimen hosta.

H. St. Paul

A stately hosta specimen in any garden, the rugged, beautifully textured and colorful foliage of this big beauty is outstanding. A wide edge in deep green surrounds a lighter green leaf center, with large, flattened leaves that sprawl magnificently to create a wonderful show. An old-fashioned beauty that I find myself drawn to more strongly every year.

H. *Embroidery*

One of those unusual plants that you either love or hate, my passion for this stunning beauty is divine. Unusual, unruly, somewhat wacky in appearance, Embroidery is one unique hosta. Every plant I have seen is slightly different. Some sprawl smooth and wide in form while others stand more upright and are more ragged in appearance. The embroidered effect along the leaf edge is quite unusual and spectacular when viewed in detail.

H. *Alligator Shoes*

A fitting name for this wonderful hosta with its over-the-top corrugation and leathery feel, Alligator Shoes stands tall in the garden with beautiful blue-green and gold leaves. It takes a few growing seasons for the intense seer-suckering to begin to appear, but the wait is well worth it for the spectacular presence and beauty the plant provides in the garden.

H. *Prairie Moon*

Soft, pale, glowing like the moon, this wondrous, flowing beauty is pure joy. Even at night, the shimmering glow of soft yellow foliage stands out in the garden. Smooth and silky with prominent veins, Prairie Moon is one beautiful hosta.

H. *June Fever*

Colorful and effervescent, June Fever combines bright, emerald green with streaks of darker coloration feathering in toward the center of the leaf. The beautiful coloration, like stained glass, does best in shade. The colors tend to fade in more sun. A striking sheen, almost always present, glosses the colorful leaves to create an elegant appearance.

H. *Blue Mouse Ears*

The classic mini that heralded the mouse ear craze, this plant never goes out of style with its cute, mouse ear foliage in thick, rubbery blue, tiny flower stems and versatile nature. Use this plant in containers of all sizes, miniature gardens, rock gardens and borders where its beauty in miniature can be best displayed.

H. *Royal Flush*

A dramatic plant in shades of yellow and green, Royal Flush is another underused and underappreciated beauty that deserves a wider audience. Its colorful leaves, often held horizontally, are gold with a brighter green center, patterned variably from leaf to leaf, layered in several shades of green and olive. The overall effect of a large clump in all its glory is outstanding.

H. *Stained Glass*

Among the most popular of all hosta varieties, Stained Glass has many outstanding characteristics, including glossy foliage, spectacular flowers, wonderful fragrance, and, of course, beautiful coloration. With more sun, the plant becomes a beautiful amber yellow, slightly washed with orange and gold, with a thin, deeper green edge. With more shade, the overall chartreuse color of the leaves and wire edge in darker green is also quite impressive.

H. *White Feather*

Love it or hate it, White Feather deserves a place among my favorites for its unusual nature, challenge in cultivation and its bizarre spring display. Emerging nearly pure white or creamy yellow, the plant retains its coloration for several weeks before slowly misting and flecking with green. Some specimens retain the white coloration for almost the entire season, a unique and wonderful effect in the garden. While it has a reputation of being a tough one to grow, I've had much luck with these plants in my home garden.

H. *Solar Flare*

Massive and show-stopping in heavily veined golden yellow, Solar Flare is a powerful beauty that dominates the garden from spring through fall. Its immense size, wonderful texture and shape, as well as stunning coloration make this a wonderful standalone specimen, or colorful companion to hostas in rich blue or deep, dramatic green.

H. *Obsession*

The subtle variegation that whispers within this unusual and often overlooked plant captures the eye as it gently shimmers in the shadows. One of the darkest hosta varieties available, in beautiful blackish-green, barely noticeable streaks both light and dark dress this understated beauty. The unique texture and substance of the leaves adds to its allure.

H. *Potomac Pride*

The obsidian gloss of this near-black beauty creates an unusual display in the garden. Retaining its rich, dark color best in the shade, Potomac Pride will brighten to a deep, shiny green with more sun. Always shimmering, always wonderfully glossy and slightly unruly, there's nothing else quite like it.

H. *Captain Kirk*

With powerful contrast in bright lime with a deep, dark edge, this plant is a beauty in the shade garden. Like many hostas, the beautiful central color fades to cream or white in more sun, so keep this one in shade for the best display of its high contrast hues.

H. *Squash Casserole*

A widespread beauty in loosely corrugated lime with nicely rippled edge, Squash Casserole is a massive specimen plant. Its unusual coloration, even brighter in the sun, along with its relatively low-growing style make this a magnificent specimen when given room to fully shine.

H. *Ripple Effect*

One of my newer favorites, this beautifully rippled and undulating, medium-sized hosta with thick, rubbery leaves and gorgeous coloration is wonderful for small beds and containers, where the wonderful effect of its namesake rippling can be best observed.

For the most intriguing coloration, keep the plant in a bit of shade. This will help magnify the rich greens, golds and blues that fade to creamy white and green in more sun.

H. *Triple Ripple*

Another hosta that completely excited me the first time I saw it on display, this one features large, heart shaped leaves with a thin wire edge in cream or chartreuse, along with elegant, heavy rippling along the leaf edges. With tall, stately stems, large leaves held horizontally and the beautiful contrast between the leaf edge and interior, this is an elegant and unusual hosta.

H. *Stitch in Time*

Famously touchy, but extremely beautiful, Stitch in Time features brilliant, lime green leaves with a thin, stitched interior in deep forest green. The effect on a mature plant is breathtaking. Unfortunately, this beauty has a reputation of being difficult to grow. Many plants either revert to a solid green, or mysteriously shrink away and disappear within a few seasons. If you've got a happy specimen, allow it to grow and thrive where planted.

H. *Montana Moonshine*

A beautiful plant that can be spotted from across the garden, the rich green and gold of this exceptional plant sets it apart from others in the Montana family. This variety has extremely wide, gold edges with just a small flare of feathered green through the center of each leaf at maturity. The intense gold color and long, pointed leaves make this a standout selection, if you can find it.

H. *Purple Haze*

A subtle glow of purple and bronze shimmers over the leaves of Purple Haze for much of the season. The effect is highly unusual, especially where the coloring is concentrated near the leaf interior and along the stems. As the purple sheen fans out across the leaf surface, it gleams in dappled sunlight in the shade garden.

H. *Striptease*

A classic sport of Gold Standard, Striptease has given rise to dozens of new varieties, many featuring the distinct central variegation pattern and thin lightning stripes that gives the plant its name. Striptease is a beautiful specimen with lighter leaf center bordered in muted gold with lightning flashes of white and cream along each side of this edge.

H. *Krossa Regal*

An old standard still in high demand, this elegant beauty with its long, flag-like leaves colored rich aquamarine in the right light, massive, vase-shaped form and towering plumes of beautiful flowers remains among my favorites. An excellent specimen anywhere in the garden, including mass plantings as a hedge of sorts, as well as in large urns or containers, the wonderful upright form works to its advantage.

H. *Silver Lode*

Fun and elegant in twisted and curled silvery green with a deeper edge, Silver Lode is a low-growing, medium-sized plant that brings its beautiful sheen to the summer garden. I prefer to grow this plant in the shade, where the silvery gleam of its center remains. With more sun, this wonderful gloss fades to white.

MAKING HOSTA MAGIC

Making magic happen in the garden provides endless opportunity for you to explore the art of combining your favorite hostas with other beloved plants, such as bulbs, trees, shrubs, annuals and perennials to create a masterpiece of color, size, texture, form and beauty. Painting your landscape with a selection of fine colors, textures and growth forms creates an ever-changing tapestry of foliage and flower throughout the seasons.

Because of their outstanding attributes, hostas make the perfect companion for many garden favorites.

Perennials, such as coral bells, lilies, ferns, native wildflowers, bleeding hearts, hellebores and others are wonderful.

Spring blooming bulbs like daffodils, tulips, hyacinths and fritillaria, as well as allium, are perfect plant partners.

Shade-loving trees and shrubs, such as hydrangeas, serviceberry, tricolor beech, miniature and dwarf conifers and others can be used to provide vertical interest and height, as can some of the shade tolerant ornamental grasses.

On the following pages, you'll find many wonderful examples of hosta companions and inspiration to help you design elegant garden showpieces using hostas and your favorite garden plants to create magic in the garden.

Spring bulbs, such as daffodils, tulips, hyacinths, fritillaria and snowdrops make wonderful hosta companions early in the season. Expanding hosta growth serves to hide bulb foliage throughout spring and early summer before it goes dormant.

H. Liberty wakens among a sea of colorful daffodils in May.

Martagon lilies in many colors tower among hostas during late May and June.

Breathtaking in foliage and airy in bloom, the many varieties of coral bells make perfect plant partners when combined with hostas in all colors, textures and sizes.

H. Gunther's Prize is paired with a rich, deep purple coral bell for a stunning display.

The colorful combination of rich purple coral bells and the stunning turquoise blue of H. Halcyon in deep shade are wonderfully displayed in this bed of layered, repeat plantings.

Colorful coral bells in shades of orange, caramel, melon and other tropical shades combine with hostas in contrasting blues and deep greens to spectacular effect.

This incredible display of decorative violets, ferns and hostas in shades of blue is as richly elegant and lovely as they come.

H. Captain Kirk provides a colorful and striking backdrop for dazzling painted fern.

Like Japanese painted fern, harder to find Ghost fern provides rich texture and elegant beauty when combined with hostas of just about any shade.

The delicate beauty of northern maidenhair graces this bed of assorted small and miniature hostas.

The incredible beauty of tri-color beech, a lovely understory tree, provides a sparkling curtain of color as it sprawls loosely over a sea of hostas in blue and deep green.

The magnificent foliage and blooms of bleeding hearts are elegant companions to hostas in full to part shade. Here, H. Ebb Tide wanders among the lacy foliage of a gold-leaved bleeding heart.

H. Praying Hands and fringed bleeding heart forever waltz together in this eternal pairing.

Shade-loving Astrantia, or masterwort provides jewel-like bloom that rises above
the colorful hostas below. This plant blooms in many shades of red, pink, purple and white.

The rich, fern-like foliage of Black Lace elderberry sprawls wildly over the brilliant gold of H. Key West. The unusual, purplish-black foliage of this fine elderberry is perfect when paired with hostas in bright gold, as well as those in blue.

Shadows and light. Two shade lovers, H. Gunther's Prize and Japanese forest grass, prove that even hot afternoon sun won't prevent the pairing from creating one of the most stunning garden combinations.

H. Kaleidochrome sprawls beautifully over a sea of variegated groundcover violets.

Pagoda dogwood Golden Shadows whispers above a sea of blues and rich greens.

What an unusual but striking combination! H. Patriot's Fire gleams over a wonderfully textured clump of Toffee Twist carex.

A delicate cloud of richly colored euphorbia or cushion spurge drifts
over a turquoise sea of hostas in bright blue.

CREATING CONTAINER JOY

You'll never look at hostas the same once you begin growing these incredible plants in containers.

Many hosta growers have yet to discover the pleasures, wonders and surprises that come with growing hostas in pots.

One of the most joyful discoveries you'll make when experimenting with growing hostas in containers is a new appreciation for even the simplest and most common of plants. Some of the most stunning and impressive hostas for containers are old-fashioned stalwarts such as Francee, Antioch, Gold Standard and others.

Hostas work excellent in containers, either on their own, or in combination with any number of annuals, perennials, succulents and other plant choices.

Many hostas lend themselves perfectly to container plantings, especially those that feature an elegant, upright growth habit or classic vase shape. Others that feature cascading and sprawling foliage are also wonderful choices.

With foliage that appears to be painted or brushed in wonderful colors, excellent shape, form and eye-catching textures, hostas make wonderful companion plants in containers and pots of all sizes, including hanging baskets.

The large number of small and miniature hostas also make spectacular container specimens, especially in miniature gardens and hypertufa planters.

Hostas such as Praying Hands, Hands Up, Krossa Regal, Regal Splendor, many of the Montana varieties and others make wonderful vase-shaped beauties that proudly display their form when placed in containers and urns.

Hostas with red stems and petioles also make wonderful container specimens. This includes plants such as Fire Island, Blueberry Muffins, Designer Genes, Volcano Island, One Man's Treasure, Rocket's Red Glare and others.

Plants with cascading leaves make an excellent choice with their draping foliage in flowing curtains of color. Examples include Cool as a Cucumber, Jade Cascade, Ringtail, Ebb Tide, Cascades and others.

Unusual specimen hostas like Ripple Effect and Whee are fun, lively plants that create breathtaking new looks when placed in pots.

During winter, container planted hostas can be stored in a number of ways. Some gardeners choose to plant in plastic nursery liner pots that can be lifted from expensive containers and stored over winter outdoors. Gardeners may choose to bury containers in compost piles, dig container plants into the garden in the fall, trench, or simply allow to remain outside the entire season.

A simple, yet elegant collection of hostas in terra cotta containers.

H. Liberty shines in a brilliant, yellow container echoed with sparking begonias in the same shade with rich, deep purple coral bells below.

In glazed cobalt, H. Wide Brim, though quite common, takes on a whole new look, both elegant and sophisticated.

Vintage hosta in wonderful shabby chic.

HOSTA DREAMS

Combining and designing to create hosta dream gardens

A perfectly combined planting of shade loving perennials, ferns and breathtaking hostas.

Hostas of many sizes and colors adorn this stacked limestone wall.

This massive specimen of H. Mountain Snow is truly a regal beauty to be proud of.

A calming sea in soothing shades of blue.

The art of hostas.

DANCING IN THE RAIN

Fresh-fallen rain, gleaming in diamond, sparkles upon the sprawling leaves of a sea of hostas that dances through the dappled sunlight of early morning.

These quiet summer mornings, ringing with birdsong and drenched with last night's rains, set the hosta grower's heart aflutter.

A silvery sheen glazes our favorite plants, condensing into metallic beads of sparkling rainwater that cling to the richly textured, colorful foliage of these sprawling giants.

As the morning sun dances through the trees, we stroll among our lovelies, admiring the short-lived extravaganza of hostas in the rain.

Sequined and glittered with droplets of moisture, our treasured keepsakes are dressed in a whole new light. Shimmering. Gleaming. Ever in motion as the canopy flutters overhead, casting its shadows upon the widespread ocean of blues, greens and gold below.

The breath of early morning drifts through the trees as the warming sun graces the shadows below.

A hummingbird dances among the lavender spires of bloom, busily darting among a forest of hosta flowers.

I love these early mornings blessed with hostas in the rain.

Made in the USA
Middletown, DE
16 May 2019